Understanding
My Gecko

Reptiles are becoming very popular pets and are overtaking cats and dogs as household members, however, their husbandry requirements are much more complex to keep them happy and healthy.

As a company who sees every day the shortfalls in caring for these specialised animals, we are pleased to endorse the series of "Reptiles are Cool" written by Siuna Reid, an experienced exotic veterinarian who cares enough to try and make a difference.

These books are very basic and provide simple steps and explanations of how and why we need to provide specialised environments for our pet reptiles to improve their captive quality of life as best we can.

—Pinmoore Animal Laboratory Services

REPTILES ARE COOL

Understanding
My Gecko

Siuna A Reid
BVMS Cert AVP (ZM) MRCVS

Edited by
Jen L Campbell
BVMS MRCVS

Vinnee

Under my skin,
deep within my heart
and entwined in my soul.

CONTENTS

Siuna A Reid

INTRODUCTION

I have been a vet for a long time and I have seen many changes in the kinds of animals that I treat. Over the past ten years there has been a huge increase in the number of reptiles that are kept as pets.

Reptiles are very different from mammals. The purpose of this book is to try to explain these differences and why they are important to the health and wellbeing of pet reptiles.

There are hundreds of different species of geckos being kept as pets. The onus is on the supervising adult to research the specific requirements before buying their pet. This book explains the importance of husbandry and some of the diseases that can occur if basic needs are not fulfilled.

Reptiles carry many different bacteria, one of which is salmonella. Although not harmful to them the bacteria can cause illness in humans. Therefore, it is essential to wash your hands after handling all reptiles.

Later in the book you will come across the following symbols. Each one highlights a particular aspect of your reptile's care, relating directly to the health issue being discussed.

House

 Furniture

 Heat and Light

 UV light

 Water/Humidity

 Food

GECKOS AS PETS

Buying a pet and looking after it is a huge responsibility. As a pet owner you have to make sure that your pet has somewhere suitable to live, has the correct food to eat and receives lots of care and attention. You have to notice when your pet is not feeling well and may need to be taken to the vet.

The most commonly kept pets are mammals such as dogs, cats, rabbits and hamsters. Humans are mammals too, so we generally find it quite easy to relate to other mammals and to realise when they are unwell or in distress. If you stand on your dog's paw he will yelp and you will know he is in pain. If your dog is too cold you will notice that he is shivering and if he is too hot you will notice that he is panting. If he doesn't eat his dinner you will realise that he is feeling unwell.

You have chosen to keep a gecko as a pet. Geckos are reptiles and reptiles are very different from mammals. Your gecko will not give you such obvious signals to let you know that he is feeling unwell, or too hot, or too cold, or in pain. His signs of distress are much more subtle and you will have to observe him very closely to make sure that he is healthy; otherwise his suffering will go unnoticed. You should weigh your gecko regularly as it might not be obvious just from looking at him that he is losing weight.

Many of the health problems which occur in geckos are related to some aspect of their environment or their diet. In this book we will first look at the correct housing and feeding for your gecko. Then we will go through the body systems of your gecko to find out how they work and what to look out for should things go wrong.

VISITING THE VET

At some point you may need to take your gecko to the vet. This symbol, which you will come across throughout the book, indicates when you will need to seek extra help, medicine or maybe even surgery for your gecko. Try to choose a vet who has a special interest in reptiles. Some vets take more exams so that they have extra qualifications for treating reptiles. If your local vets are not reptile enthusiasts they should be able to recommend a vet who is. If you have difficulty finding a suitable vet you could contact The Royal College of Veterinary Surgeons www.rcvs.org.uk.

THE HOUSE

 Where will your gecko live? You will need to buy a tank for him to use as his house. It is best to get the tank (and also the things that you put in it – see below) from a specialist reptile shop. Tanks made of glass or plastic are a good idea as these materials are easy to clean.

Within the tank you are trying to create a small world which copies the kind of environment your type of gecko would live in if it was in the wild. Desert species, such as the Leopard Gecko, need a dry environment. Tropical species, such as the Golden Gecko, thrive in more humid surroundings. Therefore it is very important that you fully research your chosen species so that you can create the correct living environment.

It is also important to think about where within your home you will place the gecko's house. The best place to put it is in a room that is used, like your bedroom or the main living room. Your gecko needs to be somewhere with a constant temperature. Do not put his house beside a window or over a radiator as the temperature will rise and fall too much in these areas.

SUBSTRATE & FURNITURE

Substrate is the material used to cover the floor of your gecko's house. If you have a desert species you should provide him with sand. A tropical species needs a combination of soil and moss.

You will also need to put some furniture in his house. He needs to have somewhere to hide, especially if his house is in a busy room. You can buy him a plastic cave or you can use pieces of wood or log to make a hide. Plants such as vines can also be used as hiding areas. Natural plants look good in a tank, but it is also possible to use plastic plants which have the added advantage of being able be easily cleaned.

HEAT & LIGHT

Life on Earth is supported by the sun. The sun provides heat and also light. Animals' need both heat and light to survive.

Mammals can control their own body temperature. The food they eat provides the body with energy and heat. If they are too cold they shiver and if they are too hot they sweat. These processes use a lot of energy.

Your gecko is a reptile and reptiles regulate their body temperature very differently from mammals. This is a major and vitally important difference. Reptiles are cold blooded (exothermic). This means that their bodies cannot produce heat from the food that they eat. Because of this they need much less energy from food to survive. A 100g reptile needs only 5% of the energy that a 100g mammal needs. To keep warm they need to bathe in the sun or sit on a warm rock. They have no hair, no sweat glands and do not shiver. This means that your gecko will show no obvious signs that they are too hot or too cold.

You need to provide sources of heat for your gecko within his house. This could be a heat bulb, a hot rock or an under floor heating mat. It is important that you know the temperature in your gecko's house, both the hottest and the coolest areas. To do this you will need to use thermometers around their house. A thermostat is a device that should be added to the house to control the temperature.

If you are not aware of the temperature in your gecko's house there is a danger that he could become too hot. As he cannot sweat to cool off, or remove layers of clothing as we would, he will need to try to hide in a cooler part of his tank. Providing a water bath is a good idea.

It is more common, however, for a gecko to find himself in an environment which is too cold. Cooler temperatures are unlikely to kill him, but will put a strain on his body and organs. His muscles, lungs, intestines and heart will struggle to work if they are too cold, and if this goes on for a long time it can lead to illness and even death.

ULTRA VIOLET LIGHT

 As well as producing heat and light, the sun also produces ultraviolet (UV) light. This is a type of light which we cannot see but geckos can. It affects the skin and in humans it can cause sunburn.

Reptiles use UV light to make vitamin D3. This helps to keep their bones strong and healthy and enables their guts to absorb calcium from their food. To obtain vitamin D3 he will need exposure to UV light for 12 hours a day.

If your gecko does not receive enough vitamin D3 his bones will become soft and they might even snap and break. He may develop twitchy toes caused by faulty muscle contractions.

Ultra violet light can be provided as a combination bulb or a UV tube. The tube needs to be no more than 30cm away from your gecko. Remember that a UV tube will not provide him with any heat. The bulb should be changed once a year. This is because although the bulb appears to be working, over time it will eventually stop making UV light.

WATER

All geckos need water to drink. It is important that it is clean and regularly changed. Without water his body will become dehydrated. Dehydration can lead to constipation. It may sound unusual, but if your gecko were to become constipated he could die.

Humidity is also an important consideration when setting up your gecko's house. When water evaporates it forms an invisible gas called water vapour. Humidity is a measure of the amount of water vapour that is present in the air.

In hot dry areas, like deserts, there is not a lot of water vapour in the air which means that deserts have low humidity. Rain forests are also hot but they have lots of water vapour in the air and so they have high humidity.

The level of humidity required for your gecko will depend on what type of gecko he is and therefore what type of environment he needs to live in. You can use a gadget called a hygrometer to measure the level of humidity in your gecko's house and make sure that it is suitable for him.

FOOD

Most geckos eat insects. In the wild a gecko would eat whatever types of insects he could catch, depending on the season. In captivity you will have to buy live insects for him to eat.

Most of the insects that are fed to pet geckos are mass reared. Traditionally, locusts, black and brown crickets, meal worms and wax worms have been fed. Mario worms and calci worms can also be obtained. This is a very artificial situation and we are greatly simplifying our geckos' diets by offering them only a few types of insects to eat.

All insects are very low in vitamins and minerals. When you buy your crickets or other insects from the supplier, they are often hungry and have eaten their cardboard containers. This further reduces their mineral content. You can boost the mineral levels by feeding some dry fish flakes or small amounts of greens, such as dandelions to your live food. Dusting the insects with calcium/vitamin D3 powder before feeding them to your gecko will also help. This will ensure that he receives adequate amounts of these minerals in his diet.

Don't be afraid to catch other insects, for example moths, or spiders to feed to your gecko. These will be packed full of nutrients and will be better for him than the commercially produced live food. If you catch insects from your garden make sure that it hasn't been treated with chemicals.

The frequency with which you feed your gecko will depend on his age and stage of development. It is important not to put too many live insects into his house at one time. Some of them might bite his skin, which will cause pain and damage. They can also be highly annoying and cause your gecko to become agitated and unhappy. So if he is not hungry, take the live food out and try again later. There is nothing worse than having your dinner sitting on your head!

SKIN

The skin is the largest organ of the body. Reptile skin is unique and has many functions which include protecting the body, providing camouflage and making vitamin D3. Some geckos have specialised skin on their feet with tiny ridges on the sole. These act like suckers allowing the gecko to stick to glass, so that he is able to walk up the walls of his house!

SHEDDING (ECDYSIS)

When mammals grow, their skin stretches and grows too. Reptiles are different. Their skin does not stretch with growth. Therefore, the ability to shed skin is very important to your gecko. When it is time to shed, your gecko will produce a chemical which divides the old and the new skin. At this stage his skin will look dull and bluish. He will naturally rub himself against rough or moist furniture to remove his old skin in large pieces. You will now see his shiny and colourful new skin.

13

It is important to keep a diary of how often your gecko sheds Sometimes geckos have problems shedding. This is known as dysecdysis. It is one of the most common reasons for visiting the vet.

Inspect your gecko closely after he has shed to make sure that all the old skin has come away from his body. Sometimes pieces of skin may stay wrapped around the toe area. This can cut off the blood supply and the toe may drop off!

 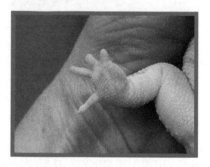

 Lack of humidity is one of the most common reasons for failure to shed. You can increase the humidity by spraying the tank with water or adding damp moss to the hide. Just make sure it is not too wet as this can lead to ulcers on the skin.

 Make sure your gecko has damp moss in his hide.

 Make sure that the temperature in your gecko's house is correct. If it is too cold he will struggle to shed.

 Any problems relating to shedding should be closely monitored and may require a visit to the vet.

SKIN PROBLEMS

ABSCESSES

Abscesses are lumps on the skin infected with bacteria or fungi. Damaged skin is a common cause of infection.

Check for sharp objects in the house.

Make sure the furniture has smooth edges.

Correct temperature will help your gecko fight off infection.

A good diet keeps the immune system healthy.

If your gecko does develops an abscess he will need to have an operation to remove it.

15

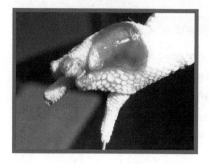

Thermal burns happen when geckos come into contact with an unprotected hot surface. This could be a heat lamp or a hot rock. Geckos seem to have difficulty detecting hot surfaces and do not react until serious damage has already been done to their skin.

Always check that any bulbs, heat pads or hot rocks in your gecko's house are working properly, otherwise they may burn him. If the heat bulb is inside the house always make sure it has a wire cage around it.

Minor burns may not need any treatment. However, serious burns will need veterinary care. This may include creams and antibiotics.

Poor diet can affect the skin. Vitamin A is very important to gecko skin. Too little of it makes the skin of the eyes and mouth become swollen. Poor sight will make it very difficult to see and therefore feeding becomes a challenge. Too much vitamin A in the diet causes the skin to become thickened and flaky.

A diet with low calcium and low vitamin D3, but with lots of fat, can result in the body growing too quickly. This leads to weak bones and skin that sheds over and over again.

Make sure you feed a balanced diet to your gecko to ensure he gets the correct amount of nutrients, vitamins and minerals to keep his skin healthy. Remember to feed his live food on greens and fish food flakes. Also dust the live food with a calcium supplement before feeding to your gecko.

To help your gecko make vitamin D3, his UV bulb needs to have the correct strength and position.

Most nutritional diseases require veterinary assistance.

EYES

Geckos have extremely good eyes that see colour and also ultra violet light.

Gecko eyelids are quite different to ours. If you look at your own eye you will see that you have a big upper eyelid which comes down to cover your eye when you blink, and a much smaller lower eyelid. Some types of gecko, such as the leopard gecko, do have upper and lower eyelids but the lower eyelid is the one which is bigger and stronger. Geckos also have a third eyelid which sweeps across the surface of the eye to clean it when they blink. However, in many types of gecko the eyelids have joined together to form one clear see through eyelid which is called the spectacle.

The coloured circle in your eye is called the iris. This determines whether you have green, blue or brown eyes. The pupil is in the centre of the iris. Your pupil will be black and round. It can become bigger or smaller depending the amount of light around you.

Geckos do not have round pupils. They are like slit like, and often the iris is the same colour as the pattern of their skin. Unlike us, your gecko can move his iris if he wants to.

Geckos have tiny bones in the white part of their eyes called scleral ossicles. These help to give the eyeball extra strength.

EYE PROBLEMS

As this photograph shows, the skin in the eye area has not shed. This causes poor eyesight and the gecko will have difficulty seeing his food.

Make sure your gecko has a hide with damp moss to help remove the old skin.

Increase the humidity by spraying the tank. Too much humidity can lead to ulcers.

The temperature has to be right. Too cold and he will struggle to shed.

If the eyelids become glued together, it will be necessary to visit the vet.

CONJUNCTIVITIS

Conjunctivitis is inflammation of the eyelids. It is often caused by bacterial infection.

 Low temperatures in your gecko's house reduces his ability to fight infection.

 Conjunctivitis should be treated with antibiotics.

HYPOVITAMINOSIS A

 A diet lacking in vitamin A can lead to swelling of the eyelids.

 Make sure you feed a balanced diet with enough vitamin A to prevent eye problems in your gecko.

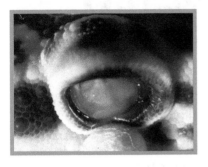

Any trauma to your gecko's eye could cause serious damage. This could happen in any number of ways. Examples would be, bedding caught in the eye or a scratch by a sharp object. An ulcer may form on the cornea. This is the transparent outer layer of the eye. Ulcers are very painful and in severe cases the eye could burst.

To prevent eye trauma you should check your gecko's house and furniture carefully for any sharp objects. Remember, when handling your gecko outside of his house care should also be taken.

Take care when selecting a UV light for your gecko's house. Inferior lights can emit harmful rays which could burn his eyes.

If you suspect your gecko has suffered trauma to his eye take him to the vet immediately. Eye damage is an emergency and if not treated in time, your gecko may lose his eye.

DIGESTIVE SYSTEM

The digestive system is the part of the body that converts food into energy. Left over waste is expelled through the vent.

The digestive tract of your gecko consists of the mouth, stomach, intestines and vent. The vent is the reptile equivalent of the anus in mammals.

MOUTH

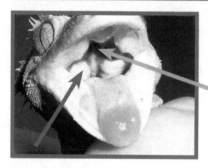

Geckos have lots of very small bones similar to teeth. When these break they regrow. In our mouths we have a roof called the hard palate. The gecko does not have a roof to his mouth. Instead he has a hole called the choana, illustrated by the orange arrow. Some geckos also have calcium glands inside the mouth, illustrated by the red arrow. These are used to store calcium. Geckos have a short, fleshy and sensitive tongue.

STOMACH

A tube called the oesophagus leads from the mouth to the stomach.

INTESTINES

After the stomach the digestive tract continues as the small and large intestine.

VENT

The vent is made up of three areas. The food waste from the large intestine is stored in the coprodeum. The urodeum is the area which stores urine, and also any sperm or eggs (depending on whether your gecko is male or female). Both the coprodeum and urodeum empty into the proctodeum, and from here all faeces and urine are passed out of the vent.

LIVER

The liver is the largest organ inside the body and has many functions. It plays an important part in the breakdown of proteins and fats from the food. It helps the body to get rid of poisons and other harmful substances.

PANCREAS

The pancreas produces juices which help to breakdown food.

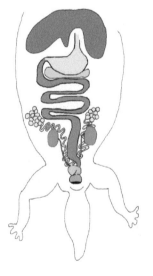

- liver
- stomach
- small and large intestine
- pancreas
- kidneys
- ovaries or testicles
- urodeum (area where urine is stored and where eggs and sperm are collected)
- copradeum (area where faeces is stored)
- proctodeum (area where all waste is stored before leaving the vent)

23

DIGESTIVE PROBLEMS

STOMATITIS

Stomatitis is inflammation of the mouth. It is commonly known as mouth rot. Stomatitis can be caused by viral or bacterial infection. It can also be caused by damage to the mouth.

Pay particular attention to the condition of the house.

Low temperatures in the house can lead to a weakening of his immune system.

Check the furniture in your gecko's house to make sure that there are no sharp areas which could damage his mouth.

If you think your gecko might have stomatitis get him checked by the vet.

FATTY LIVER DISEASE

Geckos need to eat regularly. Fatty liver disease is also known as hepatic lipidosis. Liver cells become swamped with fat, preventing the liver from working properly. It is very difficult to detect fatty liver disease. There are no obvious symptoms but a gecko with this condition will stop eating. It is important to weigh your gecko regularly to spot severe weight loss.

 Low temperature can cause loss of appetite.

 If the food for your gecko is too big, or if you feed too many insects at once, this can put him off his food.

 If your gecko loses more than 10% of his bodyweight you should take him to the vet.

25

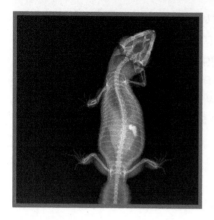

Geckos often eat the material from the floor of their house by mistake. This can lead to impaction in the large intestine. This is when pieces of material clump together and cause a blockage. Constipation is when a gecko cannot pass faeces. If your gecko is constipated you might notice him straining to pass faeces or that his faeces look very dry.

It is very important that your gecko has water at all times and that the humidity in his house is correct. Dehydration often leads to constipation.

Make sure that the material you use for the floor of the tank is large enough not to be swallowed by a hungry gecko.

Make sure your gecko is eating the right type of food and the correct amount. If he is greedy his intestines might get too full and prone to impaction.

The temperature in your gecko's house is vital. If it is too cold the intestines cannot digest food properly and can lead to constipation.

Calcium is needed to make the intestines work properly. Make sure your gecko's UV light is at the correct height and is not too old.

This condition is often left until it is too late. If an impaction is very severe an operation may be necessary to remove the material blocking the intestine.

PROLAPSE OF THE VENT

A prolapse happens when one of the organs that are plumbed into the vent, (for example the large intestine) gets pushed out of the body. Egg binding and low calcium in the diet, can cause a vent prolapse.

This is an emergency. If you suspect a prolapse you must take your gecko to the vet as soon as possible.

LUNGS

Inside the bodies of mammals there is a big sheet of muscle, called the diaphragm. This separates the chest, where the lungs are, and the abdomen, where the stomach and intestines are. Your gecko has no diaphragm. His chest and abdomen share the same space.

Partly because they have no diaphragm, geckos are unable to cough. This can be a problem because if they get a build-up of fluid in their lungs, they are unable to clear it by coughing.

LUNG PROBLEMS

PNEUMONIA

Pneumonia is inflammation and infection of the lungs. It is not common in geckos and often develops due to poor housing.

It is vital that the reptile house is kept at the correct temperature and has the correct level of humidity.

 A good diet protects the immune system.

 If your gecko is showing signs of illness then you must take him to the vet.

HEART

The heart is a specialised muscle which collects blood full of oxygen from the lungs and pumps it around the body. It also collects blood full of carbon dioxide from the body and pumps it back to the lungs. This cycle goes on continuously.

The heart sits in the chest cavity in mammals and is divided into four chambers. The right atrium collects blood full of carbon dioxide from the body, sends it down to the right ventricle which then pumps it to the lungs. The left atrium collects blood full of oxygen from the lungs, sends it down to the left ventricle which pumps it around the body. Blood is constantly being pumped from right to left, via the lungs and travels around the body inside a series of tubes of varying diameters. These are known as blood vessels.

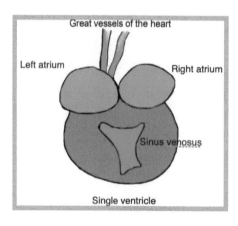

Great vessels of the heart

Left atrium

Right atrium

Sinus venosus

Single ventricle

The heart of a gecko differs from the heart of a mammal in several ways. It is especially adapted to suit the life of a reptile. It sits much further forward in the chest, between the front legs. Inside the heart of the gecko there are three chambers; the right

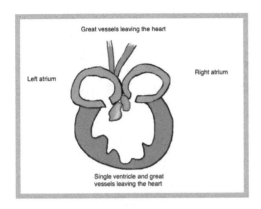

Great vessels leaving the heart

Left atrium

Right atrium

Single ventricle and great vessels leaving the heart

atrium, left atrium and the ventricle. There is also an extra chamber outside the heart, called the sinus venosus which collects blood. Geckos can move blood to wherever it is needed in the body. Remember how our mammal hearts always pump blood round the body from right to left? Geckos can change the direction of the blood so that it can flow backwards. This is one of the ways that geckos can survive if they do not have enough oxygen or if they become dehydrated.

When a house is too cold, the heart rate cannot beat fast enough to keep the blood pumping to all the vital organs.

Heart disease is not commonly diagnosed in geckos.

REPRODUCTIVE SYSTEM

The reproductive system is responsible for the production of sperm or eggs, mating, and the development of offspring. It varies depending on whether your gecko is male or female. Even if your gecko lives alone the reproductive system is still active and can develop problems.

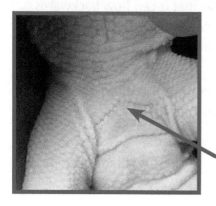

To determine whether the gecko is male or female, you need to check for obvious cloacal pores. The arrow in the picture below shows large cloacal pores. This is a male. Females do have cloacal pores but they are less prominent.

MALES

Male geckos have two testicles which produce sperm. They are inside the body near the kidneys. Instead of having one penis (willy) like mammals do, they have two. These are called hemipenes and are found inside the vent. Only one hemipene is used at a time for mating. The hemipenes do not carry urine the way that a mammals penis does.

HEMIPENE PROBLEMS

PROLAPSE

The hemipenes are normally inside the vent and only come out for mating. If a hemipene gets stuck outside the body this is known as a prolapse. A prolapsed hemipene can become damaged and infected.

If you think your gecko has a prolapsed hemipene he needs to go to the vet. If the hemipene has suffered a lot of damage or has become infected he may need an operation to remove it.

ABSCESS

Sometimes a hemipene can become impacted with hard pus, forming an abscess. This is a common condition of male geckos. The arrow in the picture shows a hemipene abscess.

A good balanced diet will promote a healthy immune system, helping to fight infection.

It is important to keep his house at the correct temperature.

If you suspect your gecko has an abscessed hemipene you will need to take him to the vet. He may need an operation to remove the abscess or the hemipene. Note that if a gecko does need to have a hemipene removed he will still be able to breed, as he will be able to use his other hemipene.

FEMALES

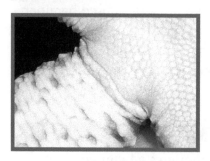

Female geckos have two ovaries which produce eggs. They are found inside the body near the kidneys. They also have two oviducts. These are tubes along which the eggs are transported to the urodeum area of the vent. Geckos tend to lay one or two rubbery eggs at a time. If they susccessfully mate with a male gecko the eggs will hatch approximately 40-60 days later. However, female geckos can produce eggs without mating and sometimes this can lead to problems.

EGG PROBLEMS

FOLLICULAR STASIS AND EGG BINDING

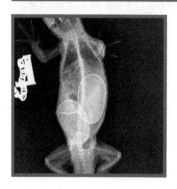

Follicular stasis is a condition where the eggs do not develop properly and are without a shell. These undeveloped eggs remain inside the body and can make an affected gecko very ill.

34

Egg binding is more common in geckos. Here the eggs have been made and are fully developed but they become stuck inside the body and cannot be laid. The picture shows an egg bound gecko.

Making eggs uses a large amount of energy. Ensure that your gecko has an adequate and balanced diet.

The house must be kept at the correct temperature. If it is too cold her body will struggle to make and lay eggs.

Your gecko will need a hiding place in her house with plenty of substrate. This allows her to dig holes where she will bury her eggs.

Dehydration will make it very difficult for your gecko to make and lay eggs.

If your gecko develops any egg related problems she will need to visit the vet. Egg bound geckos need an operation to remove the retained eggs from the body. Follicular stasis can only be corrected by spaying. This is an operation to remove the ovaries and oviducts.

KIDNEYS

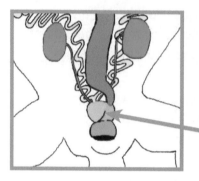

Mammals and geckos have two kidneys. The purpose of the kidneys is to remove poisonous waste material from the body.

THE MAMMAL KIDNEY

All fluid taken in by the body is processed by the kidneys. These include cups of tea, soft drinks and of course water. The kidney ensures that there is enough water to keep the body hydrated. Any water not required is stored in the bladder until it is passed as urine, which is a clear and yellow liquid.

THE REPTILE KIDNEY

The kidney of the reptile is different as it does not have the ability to retain water within the body. Reptile urine is a mixture of water and a solid white material called uric acid. The gecko has developed unique ways to keep his body hydrated.

There is a small flap inside the urodeum that can move water into the large bowel where it is reabsorbed into the body. The arrow points to this flap. The gecko can also suck water up through the vent whilst bathing. Some types of gecko have a bladder, but most do not. Their urine is stored in the urodeum and passes out of the body through the vent.

KIDNEY PROBLEMS

Gout is a condition caused by too much uric acid in the body. The uric acid presents itself as solid white material which can easily be spotted in the urine. Sometimes these hard crystals deposit themselves in the muscles, joints and organ causing damage.

 Feed a balanced nutritious diet to your gecko to prevent gout.

 Make sure your gecko always has enough water to drink. Dehydration can contribute to the development of gout.

 Gout is serious and will need veterinary treatment.

KIDNEY FAILURE

Many different diseases affect the kidneys. These include infections, inflammation and toxic damage. A gecko with kidney failure will be less active than usual, lose his appetite, suffer weight loss and become dehydrated.

The house must be at the correct temperature.

 Your gecko needs to have access to drinking water.

 Correct diet is important. Do not be tempted to feed cat food to your gecko, as this could damage his kidneys. Do not over dust the insects with calcium powder as this can damage the kidneys. A good diet also helps to support the immune system.

 Any weight loss or change in eating habits needs a visit to the vet.

NUTRITIONAL DISEASE

Nutritional diseases are caused by incorrect diet. They can occur if fed too much or too little of the nutrients, vitamins and minerals needed to maintain good health. Nutritional disease is a common problem seen in geckos, yet it is preventable.

MALNUTRITION

Malnutrition is a result of an incorrect diet. This may be too much or too little of any food. The photograph above shows a gecko suffering from malnutrition.

Make sure you feed a varied diet to your gecko.

Keeping your gecko at the correct temperature helps his stomach and small intestine to absorb all the nutrients from his food.

Your gecko needs a good source of UV light to help his body absorb calcium from the intestine.

 Most cases of malnutrition need specialist veterinary care.

VITAMIN A DEFICIENCY

 Vitamin A is needed to keep the insides of the mouth, eyes and kidneys working. Lack of this vitamin can cause thickening of the eyelids, as shown in the photograph above. It can also lead to kidney failure.

VITAMIN D3 AND CALCIUM DEFICIENCY

 Vitamin D3 and calcium are needed to keep your gecko's bones strong and his muscles active. An insufficiency will lead to the bones becoming soft and bendy. They may even break. The gecko in the picture has soft jaw bones. He cannot close his mouth.

40

 Make sure you feed a varied diet to your gecko.

 Keeping your gecko at the correct temperature helps his stomach and small intestine to absorb all the nutrients from his food.

 Your gecko needs a good source of UV light to help his body absorb calcium from the intestine.

 If your gecko has a nutritional disease he may have to visit the vet for vitamin injections.

PARASITES

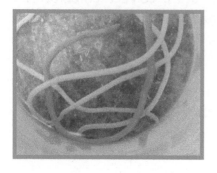

Parasites are creatures that feed off another animal. There are two basic types of parasites. Internal parasites live inside the body. External parasites live on the outside.

One example of an internal parasite is roundworm as seen in the photograph above. Roundworms and tapeworms are found inside the intestines. Mites and ticks are external parasites that suck the blood and bite the skin.

If you see any moving black or red dots on your gecko's skin, or worms in his faeces, you need to take him to the vet. These are signs of parasites.

GROWTHS

This photograph shows a swelling on the side of the head.

If you find any lump or swelling on your gecko take him to the vet. To find out exactly what the growth is the vet may need to do some tests. It might be a tumour and some tumours are types of cancer that can spread. However, the lumps may be abscesses or cysts. Some growths can be surgically removed.

TRAUMA

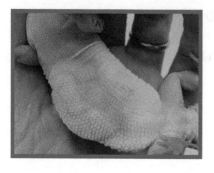

The gecko in this picture was dropped. The muscles of his abdomen have torn and the intestines have fallen out. You can see them just under the skin. He will need an operation to replace the intestines and repair the torn muscles.

Geckos are very small and relatively fragile. You must always take care to handle your gecko carefully and gently.

Injury to a gecko may also result in broken bones. Any injury will cause distress and pain.

If your gecko has suffered any trauma or injury he must be taken to the vet to be checked and to receive any necessary treatment.

AUTOTOMY

Autotomy is the ability to drop or shed the tail. A gecko can do this if he is handled roughly or if he feels threatened. The tail will eventually grow back, but it will tend to be smaller. It will also be a slightly different colour.

However, if the tail falls off very close to the back legs there is a chance that it will not grow back.

This is another reason to make sure that your gecko is always handled with care.

Any serious injuries need to be checked by the vet

NEUROLOGICAL DISEASE

The brain and the spinal chord in geckos are similar to those found in mammals. There are disease processes that affect the nervous system but these are not common. Enigma Geckos are prone to a disease of the brain and spinal chord called The Enigma Syndrome. The symptoms of this disease are fitting, not eating, and constant circling.

INDEX